OUR FATHER

Peter Tonna

All rights reserved. No part of this book may be reproduced, or stored in a retrieval system, or transmitted in any form or by any means, electronic, mechanical, photocopying, recording, or otherwise, without express written permission of the author. It is illegal to copy this book, post it to a website, or distribute it by any other means without permission.

The author has no responsibility for the persistence or accuracy of URLs for external or third-party Internet Websites referred to in this publication and does not guarantee that any content on such Websites is, or will remain, accurate or appropriate.

Scripture quotations taken from the Holy Bible, New International Version® NIV® (unless otherwise stated) Copyright © 1973, 1978, 1984, 2011 by Biblica, Inc.™
Used by permission. All rights reserved worldwide

ISBN: 978-0-6450264-2-9 (e-book)
ISBN: 978-0-6450264-5-0 (Paperback)

Copyright © Peter Tonna 2022
Published by PoeteBooks
poetebooks@gmail.com
www.ourfather.com.au

Contents

Foreword 5
Who Is God? 13
God Is Not Distant 21
God And Friendship 31
Who Is Jesus? 37
Jesus Is the Way 45
Sin And Justice 51
Mercy And Grace 59
God Is Love 67
God Understands 77
A Father's Love 85
God's Sacrifice 95

Foreword

See what great love the Father has lavished on us, that we should be called children of God! And that is what we are! (1 John 3:1)

Do you see God as distant and angry? Are you fearful of calling out to Him because you haven't before? You may think you have strayed too far and done too many bad things. You may assume God doesn't want anything to do with you. Perhaps you prayed to God but didn't receive His answer. Maybe harsh condemnation from judgmental Christians has tainted your view of God, and because of them, you believe that God hates you and there is no chance of reconciling with Him. Perhaps your parents turned you off God. Some view God the way they view their parents—their father, in particular. Maybe you were abandoned by your father, or he was abusive toward you or other family members. You assume God must be like that as well.

On the other end of the spectrum, you might see God as a cosmic teddy bear that overlooks all the wrongdoings of humanity as long as those infractions don't violate your own standard of wrongness.

Truthfully, God is neither of these extremes. He cannot turn a blind eye to wrongdoing and be indifferent to what is right and wrong. God is just and fair. He must address injustice, no matter how minor. He's no vengeful tyrant, either. He is not waiting for the next moment you commit wrongdoing so He can hurl thunderbolts down from Heaven. Yes, God is just. He is also good and merciful, which I will unravel in this book. God is for everyone. It doesn't matter how far you have strayed from God; the wrongs you have committed can't keep you from Him. If you have never reached for God, know He is waiting for you. He will not force you to do it. He has given you free will. The choice is yours. He won't impose himself into your life; you must invite Him in.

Some will argue that there are many instances in the Bible, specifically in the Old Testament, where God is angry and vengeful. Yes, God gets angry at injustice and evil, as we all do, but that's not God's only character trait. When you understand the Old Testament, you will realize that God is incredibly patient, merciful and just. The key word is "just." God cannot allow evil to go unpunished. These Old Testament passages must be read contextually. It's helpful to have a thorough understanding of the environment and civilization then; otherwise, it can be easy to misinterpret the true nature of God. There was no law enforcement organization, no policy makers or government leaders. There was a plethora of artificial gods, many of whom required amoral rituals to appease them.

To briefly explain God's hardline approach: He introduced specific regulations for the people to live by at that moment in time. From a contemporary perspective, this might seem very strict or obscure. A good example that is constantly referenced is the command not to tattoo your body or get piercings. These commands should be read in the temporal context and the group of people this was directed toward. It is not referring to piercings and tattoos as we understand them today. In biblical times, tattoos and piercings were acts of self-mutilation of the body and were morbid acts of worship and sacrifice to idols. Hence, the Bible discouraged such practices. These commands were implemented due to the people's propensity to be easily influenced by immoral and evil practices. When humanity developed their behavior, just as a child improves in maturity and knowledge throughout their schooling years, God, who sees and knows the hearts of all (1 Samuel 16:7), saw that humanity was ready for a new way of faith that He had planned since the beginning. This new way of faith is introduced in the New Testament portion of the Bible, specifically when Jesus comes into the picture. It's here that Jesus reveals the true heart of God, which I'll elaborate on in subsequent chapters.

If you are a new Christian or unfamiliar with the Christian faith and want to look into the scriptures, I would suggest staying away from the Old Testament to begin with and familiarize yourself with the New Testament. The Old Testament is a historical account of the people of Israel. It has great teachings, but the foundation of a Christian's belief and faith is based on Jesus and His teachings, which are found in the New Testament. Once you better understand the New Testament, I recommend reading the Old Testament to see how the scriptures connect.

Some may dismiss the Bible's claims about God and choose to create God in their own mind, who He is and what He is like. If you choose to do this, you must acknowledge that it is a *subjective* version of God. If you create a loving God that is impersonal and indifferent to minor wrongdoing, that's all well and good. However, if another person creates in their mind a vengeful God that sends everyone to hell, this too is valid. You can't argue against their version of God unless you claim moral and intellectual superiority and monopoly on God. Truthfully, without the biblical basis for understanding, explaining, and knowing God, all other understandings of God is subjective and a mere biased opinion. Everyone must take the time to understand whom the real God is for themselves by reading the scriptures. Otherwise, you will go through life with a distorted view of God. *You will seek me and find me when you seek me with all your heart* (Jeremiah 29:13).

Some might doubt the existence of God altogether. How can we be sure God exists? No one can prove either way if God does or doesn't exist. The question, "Does God exist?" can't be proven scientifically. Rather, it's a philosophical question. If God can't be proven, then what? The next best thing to rely on is evidence. Ask yourself questions like,

"What does the evidence point to? What's more reasonable to believe?" If you look into it, you'll discover a load of evidence pointing to the existence of God. Let me share a few prominent pieces of evidence.

For me, it's more reasonable to believe that…

- … All living things; plants, animals, and humans come from life (an eternal living being). It's unreasonable that life can begin from nothing or non-life. The animate does not come from the inanimate. Almost everyone would agree with this line of thinking; however, some will allow for the exception of the first instance of life and call it a miracle. The problem is a miracle requires a miracle-maker. Miracles don't happen within the laws of nature unless there is someone or something to control it.
- … Order and design come from an intelligent mind. You don't get complex order and design by chaos or chance. Our world, our galaxy, and the universe are intricately designed. So many components had to align perfectly for life to exist on this planet. Ask yourself this question, "Is it reasonable to believe that a hurricane passing through an airplane junkyard could leave in its wake a fully functional Boeing 747 jet airplane ready for take-off?" If your answer to that is, "No, that would be unreasonable." Then how could the universe, the world, human

beings, and everything else in creation, which are infinitely more complex than a Boeing 747, come into existence by chance?
- … For absolute morality to exist, there must be a mind prior to the human mind that defines good and evil, right and wrong. If there is no mind prior to the human mind, then good and evil, right and wrong are human constructs. Morality is subjective and depends on the society, leadership or culture you live in. A point of difference is between Western and Eastern cultures.

I wrote this book for new believers—anyone wanting to better understand who the true God is. If you're an established believer, there is something to take away from this book as well, tidbits of information that you may not have known before. I open the way to God's nature, what He is like, and how He relates to you. I kept this book brief and concise so there's not an overload of theological information. You might ask, "With all the ideals, opinions, and beliefs about God flying around these days, can I rely on this book to tell me precisely who God is?" That's a good question. Truthfully, I wouldn't base my understanding of God on anyone's views or opinions. It's beneficial to gain knowledge from others, and through books and research; however, nothing beats understanding and experiencing God for yourself. How? Read the scriptures, especially the New

Testament, and enter into a relationship with God through Jesus. Going back to the question, "Why this book?" the contents are based heavily on scripture and the life and teachings of Jesus as documented in the New Testament. The biblical scriptures are the most accurate documents in antiquities that describe the nature and heart of God, lived impeccably through the life of Jesus.

It's helpful to read this book with a Bible on hand if you'd like to look up the biblical stories and references that I have not quoted in this book. If you don't have a physical Bible, you can access it online for free at www.biblegateway.com. Alternatively, you can download the Bible app for free by typing 'bible' in the App Store or via their website www.bible.com/app. My suggested version is the New International Version.

This book is inspired by a short video called "Father's Love Letter." I recommend you spare a moment to watch it. There are several versions. I suggest the 2001 version. Go to www.ourfather.com.au. Other versions can be viewed at www.fathersloveletter.com.

Who Is God?

Do you not know? Have you not heard? The Lord is the everlasting God, the Creator of the ends of the earth. He will not grow tired or weary, and his understanding no one can fathom. (Isaiah 40:28)

Several words can describe God. He is the all-powerful Creator of the universe; He is the Alpha and the Omega, the first and the last, the beginning and the end (Revelation 22:13); He is light (John 1:5); He is the mighty rock and refuge (Psalms 62:7); He is just (Psalms 50:6); He is merciful (Deuteronomy 4:31); He is compassionate, full of grace and faithfulness (Psalms 86:15). I can go on about the descriptive words of God in the Bible, but one of the best words that summarize God in scripture is, "God is love" (1 John 4:8).

Jesus said, "This, then, is how you should pray: Our Father..." (Matthew 6:9). God is also our father. My father and your father. Jesus taught the people how to pray to God through the Lord's Prayer (Matthew 6:9–13). It's the only prayer recorded in the Bible that Jesus taught the people to pray. In this one prayer, He taught how to refer to God. The very first words indicate that we refer to God as father.

God is the Creator of the universe and everything in it; He is omniscient, omnipresent, and omnipotent.

In the Lord's Prayer, Jesus didn't address God with grandiose titles. Though, we shouldn't have a blasé approach toward God either. It's essential to revere and respect God and to praise Him for all He is. But it's incredibly telling that God, the Creator of the universe, wants us to call Him and see Him as a father. In deep anguish, Jesus prays to God in the garden of Gethsemane. He opens His prayer, referring to God as "abba, father" (Mark 14:36). In the Aramaic language, the meaning of the word "abba" is a very intimate term for father and indicates a close relationship. It's similar to saying "daddy" or "papa." You might be thinking, "Jesus can say that, He is the Son of God." The Apostle, Paul, who wrote half of the New Testament, makes reference in Romans 8:15–17 that we are children of God. Heirs and co-heirs with Jesus, and that we are to refer to God as "abba, father." As such, we are all God's children, and He is our father. It's amazing that the Creator of the universe wants you to call Him father. He wants to have a relationship with you just like a loving and caring earthly father has with his child. So don't ever be afraid or ashamed to approach God or to call out to Him. He is your father; He formed you in your mother's womb (Psalm 139:13).

You might ask, "How do I get to know God, the Father, if He really is my father?" God reveals himself through His son, Jesus, who is of God and is God in human form. Jesus said, "I am the way and the truth and the life. No one comes to the Father except through me" (John 14:6). Then there's the

Holy Spirit. After Jesus' resurrection, He ascended into Heaven. In His place, God sent the Holy Spirit to dwell in His children, "Do you not know that your body is a temple of the Holy Spirit, who is in you, whom you have received from God?" (1 Corinthians 6:19). To gain an understanding of who God is, look to Jesus. Read about His life in the Gospels, what He taught, how He treated others, and how He lived. The Holy Spirit acts as a guide and teacher, opening our hearts and minds to a deeper understanding about God (John 15:26). The more you know Jesus, the more you know God the Father. Jesus said that He does what He sees the Father doing and whatever the Father does, He does also (John 5:19). Jesus said He and the father are one (John 10:30). Jesus is God in human form. The Holy Spirit is also of God and is God (1 Corinthians 3:16). The Holy Spirit is the third person of the Godhead Trinity. How do we know the Holy Spirit is a person and not just an impersonal gust of wind? The Holy Spirit is personified in the scriptures. He has feelings (Ephesians 4:30). He has a mind (Romans 8:27). He makes decisions (1 Corinthians 12:11).

You might be scratching your head right now trying to understand the Holy Trinity. How can three persons be one? And how can one be three? How can God come down to Earth in the human form of Jesus and yet be called His son? These are difficult concepts for our finite minds to grasp. We are dealing with a supernatural being beyond human understanding and intelligence. Simply put, the

Trinity—Father, Son, and the Holy Spirit—is a mystery. Here are some examples that may help you understand how the Trinity, although three distinct entities, form and are a part of one God:

- A human being. Every human being, although being one individual, has three distinct parts. The body, the soul (the soul being the mind, will, and emotions), and the spirit.
- A scientific example of how one can be three, and three can be one is water. Water is commonly understood in its liquid state; however, water is still water when it is a solid or gas. In all three instances, the chemical makeup of water does not change, just its form.
- Space in a room consists of three dimensions: height, length, and width. If you remove the ceiling or a wall, the space of that room ceases to exist. For the room to exist, it must be comprised of these three dimensions. One or two of these dimensions do not create the space.

Another aspect of God that you may find difficult to understand is how He is fully God and fully human in the form of Jesus. He performed miracles, which humans can't do, so how can He be both? Jesus is God in the sense that, while He was on Earth, He had all power yet chose to limit His power. He only performed miracles for others, never using His divine powers for himself. By not selfishly tapping into His divine nature, He truly and fully lived the human experience. He experienced human wants, human needs, human pain, human suffering, human temptations, and human feelings. That is how Jesus, God in human form, is fully human. You might argue that an all-powerful and holy God would never lower himself to become a human. I would counter-argue by saying, "Would you dare put such limits on God?" It is absurd for anyone to assume what God can and cannot do. If He wants to lower himself to the human level so He can relate to the human experience, then He can. Rather, I'm incredibly drawn to God for caring enough to experience the weakness of the human condition that we experience.

As human beings, we acknowledge our finite understanding of God, who, in part, is a mystery. However, God hasn't kept himself entirely hidden from us. He has bestowed humanity with the information and knowledge about himself that He wants to be revealed:

- Through Jesus. "The Word became flesh and made his dwelling among us. We have seen his glory, the glory of the one and only Son, who came from the Father, full of grace and truth" (John 1:14). "The Son is the image of the invisible God, the firstborn over all creation" (Colossians 1:15). "The Son is the radiance of

God's glory and the exact representation of his being…" (Hebrews 1:3).
- Through the scriptures. "All Scripture is God-breathed and is useful for teaching, rebuking, correcting and training in righteousness" (2 Timothy 3:16).
- Through nature. "The heavens declare the glory of God; the skies proclaim the work of his hands. Day after day they pour forth speech; night after night they reveal knowledge" (Psalm 19:1–2). "For since the creation of the world God's invisible qualities—his eternal power and divine nature—have been clearly seen, being understood from what has been made, so that people are without excuse" (Romans 1:20).

Although God can't be fully grasped, He is knowable and relational. It's like that with any relationship when you think about it. No matter how long you've known someone, you can't completely know that person one hundred percent. It's no different with God. If we did understand everything about God, He wouldn't be God, would He? "Oh, the depth of the riches of the wisdom and knowledge of God! How unsearchable his judgments, and his paths beyond tracing out! Who has known the mind of the Lord? Or who has been his counselor?" (Romans 11:33–34). Through what God has revealed in the scriptures and through Jesus, we can understand enough about His character, what He is like and who He is. One of the things that God has made abundantly clear is that we are His children, and He is our father.

God Is Not Distant

I am with you always, to the very end of the age. (Matthew 28:20)

You may be someone who has experienced some difficult and traumatic moments in life. You wondered where God was in those times. He felt distant. You called out to Him for help but didn't receive an answer to your desperate prayer. I won't dare try to explain, and therefore trivialize, the pain you've been through. Ultimately, there won't be satisfactory answers on this side of Heaven. Difficulties happen to everyone. No one is immune to the pain and suffering of this world, not even Jesus, the most innocent person that has ever walked the Earth. He suffered from the world's sinfulness; He did nothing to deserve it. He suffered great pain, abuse, and death.

So where is God in our pain and suffering? This is a relatively small book, so my explanations will hardly scratch the surface. There are a plethora of books that delve into the heart of this issue. Many of the bad things that happen in this world result from humanity's poor choices. God has given everyone free will. Unfortunately, many use their free will to do evil, and others suffer. For example, an addict couple caught up in substance abuse contracts a debilitating disease. After which, they have a child, passing on the disease. This innocent new life has done nothing wrong to deserve the disease; however, they will suffer the consequences of their parents' poor choices in life. Another example would be corrupt leaders of authoritarian nations. They hoard the nation's wealth for themselves and their families while the people of that country suffer, in desperate need of basic necessities.

God allows pain and suffering, but He is not causing it. The Devil is behind the evil in this world, influencing people to misuse their free will. In part, "free will" answers the question: "Why does God allow suffering?" Even those that walk closely with God are not immune to suffering. If God intervened every time an evil act was about to be committed by someone, controlling the attitudes and hearts of humans, He would be limiting our free will. It would mean we are no longer free, autonomous human beings. We no longer have a choice. God didn't create us as robots, programmed to always do the right thing. God allows us to choose whether we obey God or not freely, to love Him or to reject Him. Unfortunately, that includes the freedom to choose whether we do evil or good. Evil is the cost of our freedom in this world.

What about suffering that's not associated with our wrongdoing or the wrongdoing of others, like sicknesses and natural disasters? Unfortunately, it's part of living in a fallen, chaotic, and sinful world; all of creation suffers as a result. God takes a step back, respecting the free will of humanity. Adam and Eve were the first to rebel, and then every generation since. As a result, chaos and evil, injustice and disease, and pain and suffering are a constant in this world. Some will assume their pain and suffering is God's punishment. This is a false assumption. "The Lord is compassionate and gracious, slow to anger, abounding in love" (Psalms 103:8). Pain and suffering are indiscriminate, they can happen to anyone at any time. Jesus explains this to the crowd in Luke 13:1–5. Jesus was obedient and sinless. He was greatly loved by the Father, even He was vulnerable to the world's fallen state.

Many will use the issue of evil and suffering for their belief that God doesn't exist or that He is an angry God. I would say it's more apt to use the issue of evil and suffering to argue for the existence of the Devil. It's the Devil that brought evil into the world. He is the author of all things evil. He uses his work to sway people to believe that God is not good and is to blame for the evil and suffering in the world. Truthfully, God created a perfect evil-free world, and then He gave it to humanity. It didn't take long before humanity tainted the world by rebelling against God and, in effect, telling God to "go away," allowing evil in.

God takes the issue of our pain and suffering very seriously. He made the effort to relate to our pain and suffering by experiencing it alongside us in the form of Jesus. He doesn't just know about it. He experienced it physically, psychologically, and emotionally: physically–His body torturously abused, psychologically–taking on the world's burden of sin, and emotionally–being separated from the Father for the first time, having only known a relationship with Him. Jesus experienced worldly pain and suffering so that God could be close to you. He doesn't recline back in the Heavens and pretends that suffering on Earth doesn't exist. For me, it's comforting to know that God understands our pain and suffering. He empathizes with our pain and grief and suffers with us. He doesn't leave us to face it alone.

God is there in difficult circumstances, even when you don't feel Him. His heart breaks with yours, "The Lord is close to the broken-hearted and saves those who are crushed in spirit" (Psalms 34:18). The world is unfair, but God is fair. Nothing is unnoticed by God. He knows all and sees all. Every evil act will be brought to justice. A hopeful outcome to our pain and suffering is that God can use the evil we've been through for good. "And we know that in all things God works for the good of those who love him, who have been called according to his purpose" (Romans 8:28). Facing the burden by yourself can be soul-crushing; you may never really get through it. However, in God's hands, He will help you with what you have been through and use it to help you and others. Jesus stated the reality of living in this world, "I have told you these things, so that in me you may have peace. In this world you will have trouble. But take heart! I have overcome the world"

(John 16:33). Jesus doesn't say you *might* have trouble, He says you *will* have trouble. It's inevitable; we will all go through troubling situations, some more so than others. But with Jesus, it is easier. "Come to me, all you who are weary and burdened, and I will give you rest" (Matthew 11:28).

God promises that one day there will be a time when all pain and suffering will come to an end, "He will wipe away every tear from their eyes. There will be no more death or mourning or crying or pain, for the old order of things has passed away" (Revelation 21:4). It's heartening to know that this life is not all there is. If it is, what else is there to hope for? Especially for those who have faced unbearable evil or great injustice. A better life is promised when all suffering and evil will come to an end.

God may not always stop or change the situation you're in. Even Jesus felt abandoned by God when He hung on the cross, "…My God, my God, why have you forsaken me?" (Matthew 27:46). Yet He still trusted in His father, "Father, into your hands I commit my spirit" (Luke 23:46). Jesus trusted God was still there with Him even when He couldn't feel Him. God brought Jesus through His suffering into a resurrected life, even after all hope seemed lost. No matter your situation, God is there with you in the midst of your trials. When it seems God is distant, He is not. He is right there with you. You're in His grip, even when it's spinning out of control. He will never leave you nor forsake you (Deuteronomy 31:6). Keep leaning on Him, and He will give you peace and comfort in your hurt and suffering, He will help you through. "Peace I leave with you; my peace I give you. I do not give to you as the world gives. Do not let your hearts be troubled and do not be afraid" (John 14:27).

It can be challenging to trust in God, especially when He feels distant. In a way, it helps to have child-like faith. Little children trust their parents to take care of them, even though at times they may not understand why their parents deny or withhold certain things from them. They still trust and love their parents to do the right thing for them. Here are a couple of examples that may help explain some of life's circumstances that don't always work out the way you'd like:

> A toddler is screaming his head off to eat ice cream before dinner. The parents deny his request, and no amount of crying will change their minds. The child doesn't understand that eating ice cream before dinner will ruin his appetite. He thinks ice cream is the best thing on Earth, and his parents are just being mean. The parents ensure that he will have ice cream after he eats his dinner, but the child doesn't want to wait.

> A child pleads in exasperation. She doesn't want to be inoculated. Her parents have great compassion for her and do their best to explain that it's for her betterment. The child doesn't care. She's solely focused on the present, not wanting to feel the pain of that needle. Despite the begging pleas, her parents continue to take her to the doctor's office to get the life-protecting injection.

These examples don't equate to every difficulty in life, but rather the distress and disappointments of losing a cherished job, breaking up with the person you thought was the one, being overlooked for that promotion you worked so hard for, or your dreams and plans not working out the way you'd want.

While you may not understand why you go through pain and tragedy, you can know for certain that God is with you in these times, even when you can't feel Him near: "For I am the Lord your God who takes hold of your right hand and says to you, Do not fear; I will help you" (Isaiah 41:13). He may not stop or change certain circumstances, but He will guide and help you through them if you allow Him: "God is our refuge and strength, an ever-present help in trouble" (Psalms 46:1). As long as there is God, there is always hope: hope for a brighter day.

God is constantly watching over you. He didn't create you to leave you to face the world alone. He wants to be involved in your life. God is relational, and He wants to be your closest companion. He wants to be the first one you go to with your troubling circumstances, and He wants to rejoice with you on joyous occasions. He wants you to talk to Him throughout the day, no matter how mundane—not out loud, but in your mind and heart. He made you so that you could have a personal relationship with Him through Jesus. He gave His most treasured and beloved, one and only son for you. A son that has been with Him throughout all eternity. Who else would do that for you?

You may have been conditioned to believe that God is distant, unloving, and angry. It may have been strict religious parents, a harsh doctrinal upbringing, or constant run-ins with judgmental Christians. If this is your understanding of God, it is false. He is not impersonal and eager to punish anyone who steps out of line. He is merciful, forgiving, and loving. The cross of Jesus is evidence of this. Don't ever be afraid to approach God or talk to Him about your concerns, no matter how small. He cares for you and every aspect of your life: "Cast all your anxiety on him because he cares for you" (1 Peter 5:7). If you think you're not that important for God to be concerned with, think again. God thinks about you constantly: "How precious to me are your thoughts, God! How vast is the sum of them! Were I to count them, they would outnumber the grains of sand—when I awake, I am still with you" (Psalms 139:17–18).

You can take comfort in knowing that God, your father, is always with you, "So do not fear, for I am with you; do not be dismayed, for I am your God. I will strengthen you and help you; I will uphold you with my righteous right hand" (Isaiah 41:10). You may think you're far away from God and can't believe He wants to be close to you. You could be going through an illness and feel alone. Maybe you've never really acknowledged God and hesitate to approach Him for whatever reason. You may have suffered at the hands of another or feel isolated by the world that has given you shameful labels, doubting that God can ever love someone like you. If you ever doubt God's closeness, remember that He gave His only beloved son for you. If that doesn't show how much God desires to be close to you, I don't know what will.

Come near to God and he will come near to you... (James 4:8)

God And Friendship

I have called you friends. (John 15:15)

A friend is someone who understands and can relate to you. A friend is someone you tell all your problems to, someone you share your most intimate details with, someone who will be there to listen when you need to speak your heart. No one will understand you more than your heavenly father. God will be as close to you as you want to be with Him, "Come near to God and He will come near to you" (James 4:8). He won't force His way into your life. Like any relationship, both parties must be willing, not coerced, to enter into that relationship: "Here I am! I stand at the door and knock. If anyone hears my voice and opens the door, I will come in and eat with that person, and they with me" (Revelation 3:20).

    Almighty God wants to be your closest friend. God is someone that will never leave you nor forsake you (Hebrews 13:5). God knows everything about you, what's happened to you and what's happening in your life right now. There is no one that knows you more than God. He knows when you sit down and rise up, He knows all your thoughts and your ways (Psalms 139:2–3). God even knows the number of hairs on your head (Matthew 10:30). It's amazing that the Creator of the world and everything in it, the master of the universe, the all-powerful and ever-living God, wants to be your close and most intimate friend. What an amazing privilege it is that God wants us to call Him father and friend: "Abraham believed God... and he was called God's friend" (James 2:23).

You may have had a rough life. Perhaps you've been neglected, mistreated, rejected, or abandoned. Maybe you've felt worthless or unwanted. These actions and words are not reflective of your heavenly father. He wants you and loves you. You are not a mistake or an accident. God has a plan for your life, you wouldn't be alive otherwise: "You are fearfully and wonderfully made" (Psalms 139:14). If you think God doesn't care about you or has forgotten you, you are mistaken. He said, "Can a mother forget the baby at her breast and have no compassion on the child she has borne? Though she may forget, I will not forget you! See, I have engraved you on the palms of my hands" (Isaiah 49:15–16). Isn't that amazing? To see how intimately God, our father, cherishes each and every one of us. Don't ever doubt God's desire to be friends with you. He knows exactly who you are and every detail of your life.

You might ask, "How can I be friends with someone like God?" Well, you come to God through Jesus. When you do that, it opens the way to the father (John 14:6). Once the relationship has been established, talk to God as you would your best friend. Go to a quiet place or go for a walk, whatever you're most comfortable with, and just talk to God as you would your best friend. Not necessarily out loud, but in your heart, mind, and spirit. Tell Him your wants and needs, thank Him for the good things in your life, ask forgiveness for the things you know you've done wrong, ask for wisdom and strength where you need it, tell Him the issues you're facing in life and trust Him with the outcomes. Practice being in His presence. The more you do that the more the relationship opens up. No place is off-limits in God's presence. He is everywhere. He is with you wherever you go. He's with you in your home, at your workplace, when at a party, at the football stadium…He's everywhere you are!

Strong friendships are based on constant communication and time spent together. Although God may not audibly speak back to you, there are several ways He may communicate with you:

- His Word. "For the word of God is alive and active" (Hebrews 4:12). "All Scripture is God-breathed and is useful for teaching, rebuking, correcting and training in righteousness" (2 Timothy 3:16).
- Circumstances. "In their hearts humans plan their course, but the Lord establishes their steps" (Proverbs 16:9). "When they came to the border of Mysia, they tried to enter Bithynia, but the Spirit of Jesus would not allow them to" (Acts 16:7).

- People. "And let us consider how we may spur one another on toward love and good deeds, not giving up meeting together…" (Hebrews 10:24–25). "Therefore encourage one another and build each other up, just as in fact you are doing" (1 Thessalonians 5:11).
- Prompting of the Spirit. "But the Advocate, the Holy Spirit, whom the Father will send in my name, will teach you all things and will remind you of everything I have said to you" (John 14:26). "In the same way, the Spirit helps us in our weakness. We do not know what we ought to pray for, but the Spirit himself intercedes for us through wordless groans" (Romans 8:26).

The best way to draw near to God and to know Him better is through the scriptures (i.e., the Bible). Reading about Jesus in the New Testament Gospels, Matthew, Mark, Luke, and John, is one of God's main ways of relating and communicating with us. The more we know God's ways and character, the more we won't confuse our feelings with God's leading. For example, He will never prompt us to do something that contradicts His Word.

Although God invites us to be His friend, we shouldn't assume we are equals; He is still God. Rather, the way of friendship that God invites us into is an open relationship, welcome anytime to approach Him and spend time with Him. It's a sure indication of how much God desires you and your time. It brings Him great joy when you choose to be near to Him; He rejoices over you with singing (Zephaniah 3:17).

God is a faithful friend who always wants to spend time with you. "God is faithful, who has called you into fellowship with his Son, Jesus Christ our Lord" (1 Corinthians 1:9). Although our understanding of God is not exhaustive, He has given us enough information about His character for us to understand who He is through the life and teachings of Jesus: "We know also that the Son of God has come and has given us understanding, so that we may know him who is true. And we are in him who is true by being in his Son Jesus Christ. He is the true God and eternal life" (1 John 5:20).

God's desire for a relationship isn't some shallow well-meaning assertion. He proved His intention by going out of His way to experience what we experience, to truly feel the depth of the fallible human condition of pain and suffering, all the way to the crucifixion. A friend isn't just someone who is there in the joyous times. A friend is someone who understands and can relate and comfort you in your most trying circumstances. In your darkest moments, you can be comforted knowing God completely understands what you are going through when others may not. God desires to intimately relate to you. When you consider what God has done, it's incredible. The Almighty God, the Creator of the universe, would sink to human weakness and brokenness so that He can relate to you. It's an incredible demonstration of His desire to have a relationship with you.

Who Is Jesus?

Jesus answered, "...the reason I was born and came into the world is to testify to the truth..." (John 18:37)

Jesus came to Earth to represent God, speak God's truth, and show His love for humanity. But who is Jesus really, and what does He have to do with God? Many believe that Jesus was not an actual person. A fictitious character made up by men. Let's start with the experts. Most historians, Christian or not, agree that Jesus walked the Earth over 2000 years ago in the area now known as Israel and Palestine. Apart from the gospel accounts of Jesus, there are non-Christian sources that refer to Jesus. Examples would be the writings of the Roman historian Tacitus and Jewish historian Josephus. Jesus also figures in the traditional Jewish text of the Talmud. In these external biblical texts, there's even mention of the "magic" Jesus performed. This would be in reference to the reported miracles as recorded in the Gospels. The Western world's calendar begins with Jesus' birth. It would be quite the hoax if Jesus were a myth. The evidence of Jesus' existence is incredibly robust. It would be unreasonable to dismiss that He was an actual person who lived over 2000 years ago.

So who was Jesus? Was He a mere mortal that taught great ethical and moral teachings? In the Gospels, He made numerous claims about being the Son of God. He performed great miracles, and was resurrected from the dead. These aren't the actions of a mere mortal. Are these claims all true? I've done my own research, studying biblical and extra-biblical texts. I can attest to the gospel accounts of Jesus' life recorded in Matthew, Mark, Luke, and John as accurate eyewitness testimony of His life, teachings, death, and resurrection. You may ask, "Can this be proven?" No, this can't be proven. But we can rely heavily on the evidence; faith is involved where proof is lacking. You might say, "If there's no proof, I can't accept it." I would respond, "That's not how you live your life." Whether you like to admit it or not, we live most of our lives based on faith and evidence every day. For instance, can you prove that the chef won't put arsenic in your food the next time you dine at a restaurant? It can't be proven. However, the establishment and the chef have an excellent track record, so you place your faith in dining at that establishment based on evidence. Can you prove that the next chair you sit on wont collapse? It can't be proven. However, the evidence is that chairs are made to hold a person weight. You don't inspect every chair you sit on. Rather, you put your faith in that chair to hold you up. I can go on, but I think you get my point. When you stop to think about it, it's amazing how much of life we live by faith, and we do so based on evidence, not proof. When accepting

Jesus' claims, the evidence must be considered. If the evidence points to Jesus being the absolute truth, then it would be wise to put your trust and faith in Him. I recommend you do your own research. If interested in looking further into the evidence, I recommend these books as a good start: *The Case for Christ* by Lee Strobel and *Cold-Case Christianity* by J. Warner Wallace.

Let's look at some of Jesus' claims as recorded in the Gospels. He claimed authority equal to God, "That all may honor the Son just as they honor the Father. Whoever does not honor the Son does not honor the Father, who sent him" (John 5:23). "I and the Father are one" (John 10:30). "He was even calling God His own Father, making himself equal with God" (John 5:18). Jesus claimed to be sinless when He addressed a crowd, "Can any of you prove me guilty of sin?" (John 8:46). The crowd remained silent; they had no response and could not accuse Him of any wrongdoing. Jesus claimed to forgive sin, something only God could do (Mark 2:1–7). Jesus claimed to exist before the Jewish patriarch Abraham who lived some 2000 years before Jesus (John 8:56–59). He claimed to live out the very nature and heart of God (John 5:19). These are just some of the claims Jesus made about His divinity. He is either whom He claims He is, or He's a lunatic. It wouldn't be intellectually honest to reject His claims of being God in human form and accept His teachings. Why? Because you are effectively labeling Him a fraudster and a liar. Would you want to believe someone like that? People who claim to be God, we lock up in mental institutions. Accepting Jesus *only* as a good and moral teacher is a redundant argument; it's simply not an option.

Is it possible that the resurrection was made up to create a new religion for selfish purposes? It's possible, but what does the evidence point to? The eyewitnesses had no selfish motivation to perpetuate the lie of Jesus' resurrection. They were a minority group in a deeply religious society, living under an oppressive pagan Roman government that didn't tolerate new religious movements. There was nothing to gain in popularity; this new movement was countercultural on many levels. It wasn't a religion based on self-absorption; servitude was one of the main messages. It certainly wasn't about gratification; this new religion, headed by men, regarded women as equals, deemed as valuable human beings to be respected and protected, at a time when women were considered subhuman and taken advantage of. There was no financial benefit; Jesus' followers spent their time among the destitute, and the vast majority of followers were poor and outcasts. If the resurrection was a lie, none of the eyewitnesses wavered in their affirmation of Jesus' resurrection, even in the face of brutal and intense persecution. All the eyewitnesses, except John, died a horrible and painful death proclaiming and maintaining Jesus as the resurrected Lord. They could have recanted to save their lives. A person wouldn't die for what they know to be a lie. You would think most, if not just one, would have given up the charade. Considering the evidence, the most reasonable motive why the eyewitnesses insisted Jesus was resurrected from the dead was because it actually happened.

Another piece of evidence for the resurrection is the fact that there is no grave for Jesus. All other prominent religious figures have a resting place. It would have been near impossible to keep Jesus' final resting place a secret, considering He was such a revered and respected figure among His followers. This is a solid piece of evidence in favor of His resurrection and ascension to Heaven.

God sent His son because He loves us and wants a relationship with us, to give us hope in this weary world, to show us a better way of living, and to provide our redemption while serving His absolute unavoidable justice. Our sin has separated us from a perfect and holy God. God initiated the ransom to reconcile us back to Him. This was done by Jesus' sacrifice on the cross: "For even the Son of Man did not come to be served, but to serve, and to give his life as a ransom for many" (Mark 10:45). It's like a rescue mission. He will destroy suffering and evil one day, yet He provides a way of escape for us. "… God… sending his own Son in the likeness of sinful flesh to be a sin offering" (Romans 8:3). The meaning of the word "flesh" in this passage translated from the original Greek text is "the sinful state of human beings." "My dear children, I write this to you so that you will not sin. But if anybody does sin, we have an advocate with the Father—Jesus Christ, the Righteous One. He is the atoning sacrifice for our sins, and not only for ours but also for the sins of the whole world" (1 John 2:1–2).

So, if Jesus is the Son of God and the essence of God, what is He like? There are many passages in the New Testament that describe Jesus. Throughout the Gospels you can see how Jesus interacts with others. He's loving, caring, compassionate, and patient. He is upfront about sin in people's lives, yet merciful. There is only one passage where Jesus describes himself, "Come to me, all you who are weary and burdened, and I will give you rest. Take my yoke upon you and learn from me, for I am gentle and humble in heart, and you will find rest for your souls. For my yoke is easy and my burden is light" (Matthew 11:28–30). In this passage, Jesus describes himself as gentle and invites everyone to come to Him. He won't turn anyone away. He is approachable. It doesn't matter where you are in life or how far down the wrong track you have gone, He wants you to come to Him. Receiving Jesus doesn't mean you'll have a trouble-free life. As mentioned previously, no one is immune to the pain and troubles in this world. But with Jesus, it is easier.

Jesus explains His innate closeness to God when questioned by one of His disciples. "Thomas said to him, 'Lord, we don't know where you are going, so how can we know the way?' Jesus answered, 'I am the way and the truth and the life. No one comes to the Father except through me. If you really know me, you will know my Father as well. From now on, you do know him and have seen him.' Philip said, 'Lord, show us the Father and that will be enough for us.' Jesus answered: 'Don't you know me, Philip, even after I have been among you such a long time? Anyone who has seen me has seen the Father. How can you say, 'Show us the Father'? Don't you believe that I am in the Father, and that the Father is in me? The words I say to you I do not speak on my own authority. Rather, it is the Father, living in me, who is doing his work. Believe me when I say that I am in the Father and the Father is in me; or at least believe on the evidence of the works themselves" (John 14:5–11).

If you had doubts about Jesus and the legitimacy of His claims, life and resurrection, the evidence is clear. God himself confirmed the legitimacy of His son Jesus, "As soon as Jesus was baptized, he went up out of the water. At that moment heaven was opened, and he saw the Spirit of God descending like a dove and alighting on him. And a voice from heaven said, 'This is my Son, whom I love; with him I am well pleased'" (Matthew 3:16–17). "While he was still speaking, a bright cloud covered them, and a voice from the cloud said, 'This is my Son, whom I love; with him I am well pleased. Listen to him!'" (Matthew 17:5).

And this is the testimony: God has given us eternal life, and this life is in his Son. Whoever has the Son has life; whoever does not have the Son of God does not have life (1 John 5:11–12).

Jesus Is the Way

I am the way, the truth and the life. No one comes to the Father except through me (John 14:6)

Jesus said He is the way. He didn't say a particular church or religion is the way. Not that being part of a church or a religion is wrong, they are good things in their proper place. However, when those things, or anything else, become the central focus of your faith instead of Jesus, then your faith is centered on the wrong object. Jesus is the source of all truth, *the* way, not *a* way.

Many will say it is narrow-minded to make such a truth claim. What about all the other religions and faith groups? It's not Christians that initiated the claim that "Jesus is *the* way"; Jesus said it about himself. You might say, "Well I'm more open-minded and I believe all religions lead to heaven." You may not realize it, but this statement is a truth claim too. If you stand by that statement, you are also being narrow-minded. You're practically saying that your way of belief leads to Heaven, therefore contradicting all other religions and faiths. When you look into all the religions and faith groups, there are similarities; however, there are fundamental contradictions of unique truth claims at the core. To suggest that all religions are the same is insulting to the followers of the various religions and faiths. You're saying, "It doesn't matter what you believe; it's all the same." All religions and faiths, including atheism, disagree with each other, so they can't all be right. Either they are all wrong, or one of them is correct.

If Jesus was just another teacher or spiritual guru that created a new form of religion, then you could probably argue the legitimacy of His claims; after all, humans are finite and fallible. But Jesus is not merely human; He claimed to be God in human form. This claim puts Him above all others. Unlike other religious teachers that claim to *speak* the truth, Jesus claims He *is* the truth. Even though there is a commonality between the teachings of the various religious leaders, ultimately, they all claim exclusivity. Jesus made exclusive claims, but He is inclusive. No matter what faith one pertains to, He calls everyone to himself. He gave His life for the world (John 3:16). That means everyone, not just a particular group.

Is Jesus being arrogant by claiming He is the truth? Is He being a bigot for implying that all other religious claims are false? The very definition of truth means exclusivity, absolute in its claim. When you think about it, we all hold to certain truths. Does that make us arrogant? For example, is it arrogant to believe that two plus two equals four and not three or five? Truth exists separate from belief. In other words, truth is not created; it's discovered. Two plus two equaled four even before we found the answer to that equation. If Jesus is God in human form, and God is not created—He's an eternal being—this means Jesus existed for all time; He wasn't created. This makes Jesus' claims of being *the* truth credible.

Unlike founders of other faith groups, Jesus is more than a teacher that merely points out the truth or the way. Jesus insisted He was the truth and the way (John 14:6). That is one of the main differences between Christianity and other religions. Christianity can't function without Jesus because it's all about following a person who is the way, the truth, and the life. Ultimately Jesus came as a Savior, not just a teacher.

What's the significance of the resurrection? Jesus took the sin of the world to the cross and with Him into His death, where sin is defeated once and for all. The resurrection declares Jesus' ultimate victory over sin and death by rising to life again, meaning life and goodness triumph over death and evil. The resurrection confirms the legitimacy of Jesus as the Son of God and His crucifixion as a genuine sacrifice for all humanity. If He stayed in the grave, the legitimacy of Jesus and His claims would be questioned. If there were no resurrection, everyone would die in their sins, and there would be no hope for humanity. "And if Christ has not been raised, your faith is futile; you are still in your sins" (1 Corinthians 15:17). The resurrection is imperative to the Christian faith.

Again, this is where Christianity is fundamentally different. It's based on belief in a person, and salvation through Jesus *is* guaranteed, "And this is what he promised us—eternal life" (1 John 2:25). Christianity isn't about following rules and rituals that make us acceptable to God. You are already accepted by what Jesus has done on the cross, you just need to believe it. I want to stress that participating in religious rituals are not bad things. But if they take the place of belief in Jesus, one must readjust their focus to Jesus, the central point of Christian belief.

Can't I believe in God and not Jesus? The thing is, Jesus is God in human form, so if you reject Jesus, you are effectively rejecting God. Jesus said, "I and the father are one" (John 10:30). God, speaking from the Heavens, said in Matthew 17:5: "This is my son, whom I love; with him I am well pleased. Listen to him!" Jesus explained to His disciples, if they knew him, they knew the Father as well (John 14:9—11). A relationship with God is based on a relationship with Jesus. He is God's cherished and beloved son (Matthew 3:17; Mark 1:11; John 3:35, 5:20). Think of it from a human perspective. Someone wants to be your friend, but they don't want to know your child, whom you love dearly. They reject your child and want nothing to do with your child. Would you like to be friends with that person? If you're like me, you would deny that person's friendship because they reject your child. "No one who denies the Son has the Father; whoever acknowledges the Son has the Father also" (1 John 2:23).

Accepting Jesus as Lord must be from the heart and not mere intellectual acceptance. Here's an example of what I mean:

> I work with someone that I don't like very much. I don't hate him. He seems unimportant and uninteresting, and I don't want to waste my time with him even though I don't really know him. This same coworker likes me and looks for moments to chat, even asking to catch up socially, but I never fail to come up with an excuse. I do my utmost to avoid spending any time with him. One day, I hear from another coworker that the coworker I dislike has just won the multi-million-dollar lottery. My attitude toward this person changes. I begin to chat in the office with him and accept his invites to socially catch up.

My desire to spend time with this disliked coworker changed out of an insincere motive. When he came into his "payday," I suddenly wanted to enter into a relationship with him. That's how many people treat Jesus and God. They don't want to live on Earth with Him, yet they expect to be with Him in Heaven for eternity when their time on Earth ends. It's not right to treat people this way and certainly not right to treat God this way.

Yet to all who did receive him, to those who believed in his name, he gave the right to become children of God. (John 1:12)

Sin And Justice

For all have sinned and fall short of the glory of God.
(Romans 3:23)

You might say, "I'm a good person," and I would agree with you. Most people are good, but we've all done some pretty bad things, too. If you examine your life like I have with mine, can you truthfully say that you've never stolen, lied, hated, cheated, succumbed to greed or hurt someone? You might say, "These are minor infringements. It's not like I've killed someone." But to a perfectly holy and just God, these minor infringements still taint us. "All of us have become like one who is unclean…" (Isaiah 64:6). Regardless of what you've done, God still loves you, and His love is perfect, beyond any idea of human love; it is unconditional. God's love is also just, and He cannot allow evil or wrongdoing to be overlooked. He wouldn't be a truly loving and just God if He did. Here's an example of what I mean:

> I go on a crime spree. I steal someone's car and set it alight. I randomly choose a guy and beat him up, inflicting minor injuries. I break into a small business, steal the cash they left in the register, and spend it all.

> I'm apprehended shortly after and hauled before a judge to be sentenced. Before the judge hands down the penalty for my crimes, I make a request. I ask the judge to overlook the lesser offenses and to be punished only for the greater offense.

What type of judge would overlook the lesser offenses? Not a very good, honest, or just judge. You might argue, "Yeah, I've done some bad, but I've done a lot more good. Besides, I do more good than most people." The second part of Isaiah 64:6 reads, "…and all our righteous acts are like filthy rags." This scripture suggests that no amount of good deeds will make up for the wrongdoings in your life. Sin taints us like a drop of poison taints a huge pot of water. God doesn't balance your good and bad deeds on a scale nor compare your deeds with others. If God lowered His standard to allow for minor human sins to be committed without just punishment, He is effectively allowing evil to win. A perfectly holy, good, and just God can't allow that; it would go against His character. It would taint the essence of who He is.

Here's an example of when someone does more good than bad in their lives:

I'm a billionaire. I'm incredibly successful in business. I am deemed an outstanding member of society. I constantly get involved in worthy causes, give millions away to help the less fortunate, build schools and hospitals, and lend my voice and person for many social and humanitarian causes. Overall, I've helped hundreds of thousands of people. However, behind closed doors, I physically abuse my wife, mistreat certain staff to the point of criminal offense, and I knowingly invest in a business that distributes illicit substances.

If I was found out, I hope you would agree that I should be punished for my wrongdoings and not be absolved of guilt because of my many good deeds. When you think about it, relying on your goodness is arbitrary. If being right in God's eyes is based on being "good enough", then what standard of goodness would it be? Yours, your neighbors, someone from a foreign country? If that was the case, goodness is subjective. Standards of goodness differ from person to person, culture to culture, and nation to nation. For instance, it might be an accepted practice within a certain culture to oppress and abuse minorities. Would you expect God to judge them by their cultural standard of goodness?

The only way there can be a just form of judgment is if it flows from one perfect standard. That can only be God's standard, good as God defines good. You might say, "It's unfair for God to set a standard of holiness that no one can ever reach." I would agree with you if there were no way to reach that standard. However, God did pave the way for us to attain that "unreachable" standard of holiness, and that is by simply believing in the work of Jesus Christ.

Once you were alienated from God and were enemies in your minds because of your evil behavior. But now he has reconciled you by Christ's physical body through death to present you holy in his sight, without blemish and free from accusation. (Colossians 1:21–22)

There will be times when you try your best and still fail, but don't give up. God is a God of many chances; His mercy is limitless, and His love endures forever (Psalms 136:1). God sent His most cherished son, as a sacrifice for you, and this means He won't discard you because of your mistakes. Keep trying to do your best, sincerely repent and move on: "If we confess our sins, he is faithful and just and will forgive us our sins and purify us from all unrighteousness" (1 John 1:9). True repentance is acknowledging you are a sinner and having a sincere desire to change your heart, attitudes, thoughts, and behaviors, in line with a godly way of living. "Yet you, Lord, are our Father. We are the clay, you are the potter; we are all the work of your hand" (Isaiah 64:8). As you continue to walk with God, He will continue to mold and shape you and help you in your faith journey.

A loving, earthy father won't disown their children if they make a mistake. The all-loving heavenly Father won't disown His children. God is faithful to us: "If we are faithless, he remains faithful, for he cannot disown himself" (2 Timothy 2:13). A loving earthly father wants to help their child through their mistakes, and it's no different with your heavenly father. He wants to help you too, to make you into the person He truly made you to be. Don't think you need to "clean yourself up" or reach some level of piety to call out to God. He never asks us to be perfectly put together because He knows that we are not capable of being perfect; He wants you to call out to Him as you are, a broken and flawed human being, like everyone else.

Sin separates us from God. Not only must we confess and repent for past sins, but confess and repent constantly, as we will intermittently fall into sin. Unfortunately, we will never be free of sin this side of Heaven, and so the enemy will do his best to get us to fall into sin. Be careful not to get into a habit of continual willful sin. Having a blasé approach toward sin will have a damaging effect on our hearts, becoming more and more desensitized toward sinfulness, which will bring into question the sincerity of our faith and belief.

I, even I, am he who blots out your transgressions, for my own sake, and remembers your sins no more. (Isaiah 43:25)

This book is about God, but I will make a brief mention of God's antithesis: the Devil, Satan. Satan plays a consistent part in your life and you may not even know it. In many instances, he is the reason why we sin and make mistakes. In saying that, we shouldn't shift the blame of our sins on him. Truthfully, we all play our part in the wrongs we commit. His greatest deception over humanity is to convince people he doesn't exist; that God is to blame for all the rampant evil in the world when he is the one who coerces people to commit evil acts. His chief purpose is to destroy what God loves most: you. He is a liar (John 8:44) and a thief: "The thief comes only to steal and kill and destroy; I have come that they may have life, and have it to the full" (John 10:10). If he can't destroy you, he will destroy your God-given purpose, just like he tried to ruin Jesus' purpose by tempting Him in the desert (Matthew 4:1–11). He does this by trying to break our relationship with God through the obvious sins and even the not-so-obvious sins of stubbornness, pride, confusion, and wrong desires that might otherwise be accepted by secular society. He doesn't want you to spend eternity with God, and he will attack you where he knows you're not strongest. "Be alert and of sober mind. Your enemy the devil prowls around like a roaring lion looking for someone to devour" (1 Peter 5:8). This world is full of darkness. There is pure evil behind the grotesque, abhorrent, immoral, and debauchery that affect the lives of many. Satan wants everyone to follow him into that darkness, away from the light of God. As long as you're breathing in this world, no one is immune from the attacks of the evil one. But we're not alone; God is here to help us. Our real battle against sin is from the dark spiritual forces in the world, in God's strength we can overcome them.

Finally, be strong in the Lord and in his mighty power. Put on the full armor of God, so that you can take your stand against the devil's schemes. For our struggle is not against flesh and blood, but against the rulers, against the authorities, against the powers of this dark world and against the spiritual forces of evil in the heavenly realms. Therefore put on the full armor of God, so that when the day of evil comes, you may be able to stand your ground, and after you have done everything, to stand. Stand firm then, with the belt of truth buckled around your waist, with the breastplate of righteousness in place, and with your feet fitted with the readiness that comes from the gospel of peace. In addition to all this, take up the shield of faith, with which you can extinguish all the flaming arrows of the evil one. Take the helmet of salvation and the sword of the Spirit, which is the word of God. And pray in the Spirit on all occasions with all kinds of prayers and requests. With this in mind, be alert and always keep praying for all the Lord's people. (Ephesians 6:10–18)

Mercy And Grace

But he was pierced for our transgressions, he was crushed for our iniquities; the punishment that brought us peace was on him, and by his wounds we are healed. We all, like sheep, have gone astray, each of us has turned to our own way; and the Lord has laid on him the iniquity of us all. (Isaiah 53:5–6)

If God is just by nature and we're all sinners, what chance do we have of being saved? God's character is also merciful and gracious. You might be wondering, "How does that work? The very definition of justice, mercy, and grace seem at odds with each other." Justice is getting what we deserve for our wrongdoing. Mercy is not giving us what we deserve. Grace is giving us what we don't deserve. Although these character traits of God seem to conflict, He fulfills them perfectly. He gives us grace and mercy through the righteousness of Jesus, placing our sins onto Jesus on the cross, which fulfills His absolute justice. And that's why Jesus was sent to the Earth (1 John 3:5), so the world could be reconciled to God. And to save humanity from His just punishment for their sins. "…That God was reconciling the world to himself in Christ, not counting people's sins against them..." (2 Corinthians 5:19). Jesus lived a sinless life (1 Peter 2:22) and was truly the only perfect human being to have ever walked the Earth. So yes, God's nature is just, and He must punish wrongdoing. However, in His merciful and gracious nature, He provided a way to remove the judgment that would have otherwise been on us. Only someone who has never sinned could have taken our place in judgment. So, when you put your faith in Jesus as Lord and Savior and accept His sacrifice for you on the cross for your sin, the entire penalty for your sin is effectively nailed to Jesus on the cross, and you are deemed "not guilty" because of Jesus' sacrifice. The Apostle, Paul, wrote about how the forefather of the faith, Abraham, was credited with righteousness and explains this is for us too: "This is why 'it was credited to him as righteousness." The words "it was credited to him" were written not for him alone, but also for us, to whom God will credit righteousness—for us who believe in him who raised Jesus our Lord from the dead. He was delivered over to death for our sins and was raised to life for our justification'" (Romans 4:22–25). He became your sin, and so your sin has been taken care of by Jesus, "God made him who had no sin to be sin for us, so that in him we might become the righteousness of God" (2 Corinthians 5:21).

Everyone will face judgment once their life on Earth is over. For someone who has put their trust and faith in Jesus as Savior, God will see that person as "not guilty" because Jesus took on their penalty, and they will spend eternity with the Father in Heaven. That's it! There is nothing more you need to do. It has all been done by Jesus. "For it is by grace you have been saved, through faith——and this is not from yourselves, it is the gift of God—not by works, so that no one can boast" (Ephesians 2:8–9). Grace is undeserved favor. Even more than that, grace is a person, grace is Jesus. Jesus epitomized grace by dying for us while we were still sinners, "But God demonstrates his own love for us in this: While we were still sinners, Christ died for us" (Romans 5:8). Grace can only be received through faith in Jesus. When you receive Jesus, you receive grace. As mentioned earlier, you can't earn Gods' salvation. God acted on our behalf because we could not save ourselves. We just have to believe and trust in Him. This invitation to receive God's gift of grace is open to everyone, no matter who they are or whatever they have done. "… He forgave us all our sins, having cancelled the charge of our legal indebtedness, which stood against us and condemned us; he has taken it away, nailing it to the cross" (Colossians 2:13–14).

I want to stress the redundancy of *relying* on good works to earn God's favor or a pathway to Heaven. The people asked Jesus, "What must we do to do the works God requires?" (John 6:28). Humanity ideologically believes we must be good enough to earn God's favor. Even many Christians rely on performing certain rituals and good deeds to earn salvation. There's nothing wrong with performing religious rituals as an act of worship; however, when faith is placed in the rituals to earn

God's favor or forgiveness, this is a false belief. Jesus answered the people, and informed us of what is required from God, "The work of God is this: to believe in the one he has sent" (John 6:29). That is all that's required. The work or deed we are to do is to simply *believe* in Jesus. Grace is unique to Christianity. By believing, Heaven with God *is* guaranteed (1 John 2:25). *"Therefore, there is now no condemnation for those who are in Christ Jesus"* (Romans 8:1).

You might be someone that thinks, "I've made too many mistakes, God doesn't want anything to do with me." Well let me tell you, you don't know how wrong you are! The scriptures state that *all* have sinned (Romans 3:23). Not some, not most, but *all.* Besides Jesus, everyone that has ever lived on Earth has made mistakes. That includes the people written about in scripture. The Bible is full of imperfect people, yet God still had a relationship with them. To name a few from the Old Testament: Abraham, Moses, Samson, and King David all made mistakes. God was displeased with what they did, and they suffered the consequences of their poor choices, yet God didn't abandon them. From the New Testament, Jesus' disciples all failed Him at some point. The head disciple, Peter, denied he knew Jesus to save his own skin (Luke 22:54–62). God still used Peter and the other disciples to fulfill His purpose. God used the woman at the well, a moral and social outcast, to spread the word about Jesus (John 4:1–41). She was deemed a moral outcast due to her many failed marriages and was the first female evangelist recorded in scripture. One of the most infamous characters of the New Testament was Saul of Tarsus, also known as Paul. He was a violent and aggressive persecutor of the early church and executed and incarcerated many Christians. Yet God still called Him (Acts 9:1–19) and used Him to spread the gospel throughout the known world. Paul ended up writing almost half of the New Testament. Apart from Jesus, he is the most influential person in Christian history.

One of the criminals crucified next to Jesus repented and acknowledged Jesus as Lord. We don't know for certain what type of life this man lived. Most likely he was involved in a life of crime far from pious living. In his final moments, this criminal admitted his wrongdoing (Luke 23:41), then he asked something of Jesus. He asked Jesus to remember him when He comes into His kingdom (Luke 23:42). In the eleventh hour of this criminal's life, he asked for mercy. The request was sincere; he humbled himself, repented, and accepted Jesus as Lord. Jesus acknowledged His request and responded, "Truly I tell you, today you will be with me in paradise" (Luke 23:43). With God, it truly is never too late to come to Him. "And whoever comes to me I will never drive away" (John 6:37). These are some examples of people in the Bible who have "stuffed-up" like we all do, and yet God, in His mercy and grace, still used them to fulfill His plan and purpose. It's no different with you. He can use you if you let

Him. These examples in the scriptures are to show you that God can and will use anyone regardless of what they've done or what they've been through. No one is beyond redemption from a life that is the complete opposite of a relationship with God. It's easy to feel unworthy and think that God can't use someone like you. But when you read the scriptures, you'll realize that God only uses imperfect people. That's because perfect people simply don't exist—apart from Jesus of course.

Guilt, derived from sin, can be such a heavy burden. It has a way of instilling a feeling of unworthiness. It can be intimidating, even fearful, to approach a holy God, asking for forgiveness. Don't let those feelings hold you back. The scriptures are clear: you will receive mercy and grace. "Let us then approach God's throne of grace with confidence, so that we may receive mercy and find grace to help us in our time of need" (Hebrews 4:16). Besides, God knows everything anyway, nothing you do is a surprise to Him; He already knows the wrongs you have done so you might as well admit them to Him. He is there waiting for you to recognize your sin and to confess and repent from your heart. By admitting your sinfulness, He will immediately forgive you. In Jesus, you have a new start every time in your journey to spiritual maturity.

Though sin has been taken care of by Jesus, that doesn't mean you have a free pass to do whatever you want. If you're thinking, "Sweet, I can do whatever I want now that Jesus has taken away all my sins," think again. Yes, those who have trusted Jesus as their Savior will spend eternity with Him in Heaven. However, there are eternal and worldly consequences to our actions while on Earth. Firstly, there will be a second judgment for the deeds we have done on Earth. "For we must all appear before the judgment seat of Christ, so that each of us may receive what is due us for the things done while in the body, whether good or bad" (2 Corinthians 5:10). This second judgment relates to the standing or reward we will receive in Heaven. Secondly, there are earthly consequences to sin, which can damage relationships and reputation. All relationships must be based on mutual respect, and there are boundary lines that shouldn't be crossed. A relationship won't last long if wrongdoing persists. For instance, if you've just gotten married, that doesn't mean you have a free pass to go clubbing every night with your mates, or to act promiscuously around others. In fact, it's quite the opposite; because of the committed relationship, you won't do any such things because of a sincere desire to honor and respect the relationship. Your behavior changes, not out of duty or compulsion, but out of a sincere love for your spouse. The natural by-product of every relationship is kindness, goodness, trust, faith, and obedience to each other, and it's no different in a relationship with Jesus.

In him we have redemption through His blood, the forgiveness of sins, in accordance with the riches of God's grace. (Ephesians 1:7)

God Is Love

... God is Love ... (1 John 4:8)

God is Love. Notice that it doesn't say God loves. Although He does love, God is described as being the source of all love. The scriptures specifically state that He *is* love. It is not just one of God's attributes, it is who He is. In other words, He is the epitome of all love. He is the embodiment of love beyond what our finite minds and hearts can understand. God's love is unconditional. It is vastly different from human love, which is mostly based on feelings, attraction, and conditions. God's love transcends feelings. He loves us, not because we do good things, but rather, He loves us because that is His nature.

God demonstrates His love for us in the most amazing way, by giving up His most cherished son. A son that has been with Him throughout all eternity. The Son was not created. He was there at the creation of the world. In the book of Genesis, God said, "Let us…" (Genesis 1:26). God didn't say, "Let me." The "us" reference means there were others with God since the dawn of time. This references Jesus (and the Holy Spirit) being with God, the Father, throughout all eternity. In Genesis 1:1, it reads, "In the beginning God created the heavens and the earth." The Old Testament was written in Hebrew, the Hebrew word for *God* in this passage is plural and means more than one, plural in form but singular in meaning. In the opening verses of John's gospel, it states, "In the beginning was the Word, and the Word was with God, and the Word was God. He was with God in the beginning" (John 1:1–2). Who is the "Word" in this passage? It's referring to Jesus. "The Word became flesh and made his dwelling among us. We have seen his glory, the glory of the one and only Son, who came from the Father, full of grace and truth" (John 1:14).

These passages show how the Son, Jesus, was with God, the Father, for all eternity. Jesus has never been separated from His father. I wanted to paint a picture and show how close and intimate the Father and the Son are, to show the amazing love of God to have given up His most cherished and beloved son for us. God knew that by giving us Jesus, it meant He would be separated from His son for the first time ever. Why? Jesus became our sin (2 Corinthians 5:21). God is perfectly holy and is incompatible with sin, and so He had to separate himself from His son, Jesus. Jesus cried out from the cross, "My God, My God, why have you forsaken me?" (Matthew 27:46). It's the first time that Jesus refers to His father as "God." Up until that point, whenever He spoke to God, He called Him "father." This showed that the relationship between the Father and the Son was severed for the first time in all eternity because of our sin. All Jesus had ever known was His relationship with the Father. If carrying the world's sin weren't enough, the separation from the Father would have crushed His heart even more. But His heart ached for us so much that He was willing to take on our sin and He laid down His life for us (John 10:17–18). That's the epitome of God's love.

Love costs something for everybody and it's no different with God. God gave Jesus over to a world, and the world rejected Him. We were undeserving of His mercy and grace. God doesn't love from a distance. He came down to Earth for us. He served the world by His sacrifice, the Creator serving the creation. It's undeniable that Jesus showed the greatest act of love anyone could ever live out.

Real and honest love demands free will. Without free will, it's not real love. He didn't have to give His life for us on the cross, He freely chose to. His love wasn't self-centered but selfless. Many of the people that Jesus died for rejected, abused, and mocked Him. Yet, He still freely chose to sacrifice His life for them and us. This is the height of love, and Jesus' love embraces the world. God's love is not forceful, but respectful. He does not force anyone to love Him and yet He still loves them. God's love does not discriminate, and Jesus lived it while on Earth by healing and associating with people from all walks of life, regardless of race, culture, social status, religion, gender or ability. God sent Jesus for everyone, not for a certain ethnic group or for the pious. "For God so loved the world that he gave his one and only Son, that whoever believes in him shall not perish but have eternal life" (John 3:16). The key words in this passage are, *the world* and *whoever*, that means everyone. He doesn't reserve His love for those who do better than others, those who are rich and famous, or more educated. His love is unconditional and equal to all. If you are currently part of another religion or of no religion, you are loved by God and He wants you to know His love for you. God's love is patient. He doesn't want anyone to live apart from Him (2 Peter 3:9).

God's desire, first and foremost, is to reconcile the world to himself. "For God did not send his Son into the world to condemn the world, but to save the world through him" (John 3:17). God does not show favoritism. Everyone can come to know the love of God equally through the gift of Jesus. There's no argument. God loves everyone and everyone has His love. The question is, do you want to reciprocate that love and receive the gift of Jesus? "Everyone who calls on the name of the Lord will be saved" (Romans 10:13; Acts 2:21). You might argue, "Well if God loves me that much, shouldn't that be enough for me to go to heaven? Why do I have to love Him back?" Think of it from an earthly perspective. To have a relationship with someone, particularly a marriage, affection and love must come from both people. A relationship simply can't be maintained if one person is not reciprocating the love of the other. If the one giving the love is not receiving love in return, they will respect that person's decision and will not force the other person into a relationship. It's no different with God. He won't force anyone into a relationship with Him on Earth, which flows into eternity.

"Love is patient, love is kind. It does not envy, it does not boast, it is not proud. It does not dishonor others, it is not self-seeking, it is not easily angered, it keeps no record of wrongs. Love does not delight in evil but rejoices with the truth. It always protects, always trusts, always hopes, always perseveres. Love never fails..." (1 Corinthians 13:4–8). This passage of scripture gives an excellent description of love. God is love, so it's God that is being described in this passage. I will supplement the word "God" to show you what I mean:

God is patient, *God* is kind, *God* does not envy, *God* does not boast, *God* is not proud. *God* does not dishonor others, *God* is not self-seeking, *God* is not easily angered, *God* keeps no record of wrongs. *God* does not delight in evil but rejoices with the truth. *God* always protects, always trusts, always hopes, always perseveres. *God* never fails...

Now I will answer one of the most asked questions about God: How could an all-loving God send people to hell? Firstly, what is hell? Depictions of hell are quite vague in scripture. We're not given a clear understanding. The one certain thing is that hell is an eternal separation from God. I would imagine that separation from God would not be pleasant. Hell wasn't prepared for humanity; rather, it was prepared for the Devil and his angels, "… the eternal fire prepared for the devil and his angels" (Matthew 25:41). Going back to the question, "Why does a loving God send people to hell?" He doesn't. God does not send anyone to hell. The scriptures are clear. He wants *everyone* to spend eternity with Him. That's why God sent Jesus to Earth, to get you into Heaven with Him. God, the Father, wants everyone to be with Him, "Not wanting anyone to perish, but everyone to come to repentance" (2 Peter 3:9). "… God our Savior, who wants all people to be saved and to come to a knowledge of the truth" (1 Timothy 2:3–4). It's people that send themselves to hell. How? By each person's own decision. God is not a tyrant or a bully, forcing you to live a certain way. He allows everyone to exercise their free will. Because God loves you so much, His love is the absolute form of love. Therefore, His love does not coerce or manipulate. He respects your freedom to love and live, or not to love and live, for God. If you choose to live on Earth with God, then you will live with God for eternity because that is what *you* have chosen. If you choose not to live on Earth with God, He won't force you to be in Heaven with Him because that is what *you* have chosen. It's that simple. God allows you and me to make a decision to say "no" to Him, yet He allows us to say "yes" to Him as well, making the way easy through faith in Jesus. You do not have to do impossible tasks or attain an impossible standard of goodness. The individual's choice sends them either to an eternal relationship with God or an eternal separation from God. God lets each person decide where they spend eternity. No one should be upset with God or blame Him for allowing each person to choose. In fact, He should be praised for not forcing anyone to do anything against their will. No one will spend eternity apart from God because they've been bad and sinful. If that were the case, no one would be spending eternity with God because we've all been bad and sinful at some point in our lives. Rather, it is the simple act of receiving Jesus as Lord and Savior and believing in Jesus and His work on the cross. People don't go to hell because of sin; they go to hell because of unbelief. Jesus never once said, "If you don't sin, you'll go to heaven." He does say many times, "The one who *believes* will have eternal life" (John 3:15; John 6:47; John 11:25–26). It's up to each individual if they want to receive Jesus or not, to live in Heaven with Him or not.

Jesus freely gave up His life for the world, "I lay down my life…No one takes it from me, but I lay it down of my own accord…" (John 10:17–18). He knew that most would reject and hate Him, yet out of love for His father and us, He sacrificed himself for us anyway. There is still hope, even for people who are unfaithful, spiteful, unlovable, or lost. Jesus died for such people too, and He yearns for the day they turn their hearts toward Him. His love is limitless and knows no bounds. Now that is real love!

For God so loved the world that he gave his one and only Son, that whoever believes in him shall not perish but have eternal life. (John 3:16)

You may have heard that God is jealous and think, "If God is jealous, how can His love be perfect?" It is true that God is jealous, but His jealously is totally different from how we understand human jealousy, which is based on selfishness and conceit. God's jealousy is purely based on a zealous type of love. The original New Testament Greek meaning of the word that describes God's jealousy means to have an attitude or emotion of deep concern. It's a positive form of jealousy. In human terms, if a man saw his wife being wooed by another man, he is right to be jealous. This is an appropriate and positive form of jealousy. God's jealous love wants to keep us from destruction and from anything that pulls us away from Him. That doesn't mean we can't love others; of course, God wants us to. But when our love for others reaches a point of worship, treating the one we love like a god, this can become destructive and dangerous. It aches His heart when we seek love and affection elsewhere in this world. Just like an earthly parent would be greatly grieved if their son or daughter chose to reject their love and seek the relationship of a gang leader or drug dealer that doesn't have the best interest for their child. God, the Father, is immensely troubled when we seek solace in the wrong things, even though they may seem harmless on the surface. His love strives to seek our betterment. Even when we are going in the opposite direction to Him, He never quits drawing us back to himself. You may have heard the term of loving someone to death. Jesus is the only one to have done that for you.

...To grasp how wide and long and high and deep is the love of Christ, and to know this love that surpasses knowledge—that you may be filled to the measure of all the fullness of God. (Ephesians 3:18–19)

God Understands

For we do not have a high priest who is unable to emphasize with our weaknesses... (Hebrews 4:15)

God experienced firsthand the failings and weakness of the human condition. This is where God, the Father, from a Christian perspective, is totally different when compared to gods of other religions and faiths. The main figures of other faith groups and religions are detached and distant. There's no relation and/or understanding of the human condition. However, God, the Father, came down to Earth in the form of Jesus and initiated the relationship with humanity. A good way to put it is, all other faith groups and religions are humanity's attempt to reach God; Jesus is God's attempt to reach humanity.

This is where Christianity stands out from all other faith groups and religions. God is a suffering God. He battles alongside the person in hospital fighting a sickness. He lies helpless in the gutter with the homeless. He carries the burden of a parent concerned over a wayward child. He grieves with you over the loss of a loved one. He is there in the midst of your pain and suffering. He knows, He cares, He understands.

God, through Jesus, experienced the same hardships and situations that we go through. God knows what you are feeling when you are happy, when you are sad, when you are angry, when you are in the depths of agony, distress or depression. Here are some examples of where Jesus, God, experienced the real human condition:

- **Frustration/Anger** – When Jesus turned the tables in the temple (Matthew 21:12–13); and when Jesus was angry with the people for valuing man-made laws above loving others (Mark 3:4–5).
- **Injustice** – When Jesus was unlawfully arrested and had false allegations made against Him (Mark 14:43; 55–59).
- **Abandonment** – When Jesus was arrested, and His disciples left Him (Matthew 26:56).
- **Doubt/Loneliness** – On the cross when Jesus called out to God, "Why have you forsaken me?" (Matthew 27:46).
- **Physical/Verbal Abuse** – When Jesus was mocked and beaten by the soldiers (Matthew 27:27–31).
- **Broken Promises** – When Jesus' disciples vowed to stand with Him, but then denied Him in His time of need (Matthew 26:33–35; 26:69–75).

- **Rejection** – When Jesus was rejected in His hometown of Nazareth (Luke 4:28–30). Throughout His ministry He was rejected by the chief priests, the pharisees, religious leaders, and the people. Even His own family (Mark 3:21; John 7:5).
- **Despair/Depression** – When Jesus sweat great drops of blood in the garden of Gethsemane (Luke 22:44).
- **Overwhelmed** – When Jesus asked His father to take the cup of suffering from Him (Luke 22:42).
- **Sadness** – When Lazarus died, Jesus cried (John 11:35).
- **Tested/Tempted** – When Jesus was in the desert (Matthew 4:1–11).
- **Betrayal** – When Jesus was betrayed by Judas (Luke 22:1–6).
- **Exhaustion** – When Jesus did not eat for forty days (Matthew 4:2). When Jesus walked for a long while (John 4:6).
- **Anguish/Distress** – When Jesus took some of the disciples to pray in the garden of Gethsemane (Matthew 26:36–38).
- **Defeated** – When Jesus stumbled carrying the cross and then was carried by Simon from Cyrene (Matthew 27:32).
- **Ridiculed** – When Jesus was ridiculed by the religious leaders and others as He hung on the cross (Matthew 27:39–42).

- **Persecution/Torture** – When Jesus was crucified (Luke 23:26–43).
- **Poverty** – When Jesus spoke of His lack of possessions (Matthew 8:20).

For this reason he had to be made like them, fully human in every way, in order that he might become a merciful and faithful high priest in service to God, and that he might make atonement for the sins of the people. Because he himself suffered when he was tempted, he is able to help those who are being tempted (Hebrews 2:17–18).

Although Jesus was both divine and human, His divinity didn't act as a shield against earthly pain and suffering. He endured these human conditions as a regular human being would, and entered into every detail of human life. He didn't just come in the appearance of a human, He lived the feelings, the emotions, and the psychological and physical human condition. God knows and understands exactly how you feel when you've been hurt by someone, when you're going through pain or dealing with anxiety and depression, when the pain and sadness seems unbearable. He can relate to whatever you are dealing with, not only because He understands but also because He is deeply concerned and cares for you (1 Peter 5:7). It's comforting to know we can approach Him when we endure the challenges that life throws at us. Out of anyone and everyone, He truly understands and knows our pain.

Praise be to the God and Father of our Lord Jesus Christ, the Father of compassion and the God of all comfort, who comforts us in all our troubles… (2 Corinthians 1:3–4)

God knows everything, yet He still wants you to come to Him in prayer: "Come to me, all you who are weary and burdened, and I will give you rest" (Matthew 11:28). Jesus modeled prayer beautifully for us to follow His example. He is God's very own son. God was right there in the midst of His life. Yet Jesus made a constant habit of praying. Even withdrawing by himself to pray to the Father (Matthew 14:13; Luke 5:16, 6:12). If Jesus placed such importance on prayer, how much more should we? Praying to God for specific answers doesn't mean an automatic "yes" to your every request. God is not a cosmic genie that exists to fulfill all our demands. Even Jesus' prayer for the cup of suffering to be taken away from Him was not met with a "yes" (Luke 22:42). Jesus understands the silence of unanswered prayer. You may ask, "If God knows everything and doesn't necessarily answer our prayers the way we'd like, why pray at all?" Prayer doesn't always change your situation, but it does change you, and draws you closer to God. "Do not be anxious about anything, but in every situation, by prayer and petition, with thanksgiving, present your requests to God. And the peace of God, which transcends all understanding, will guard your hearts and your minds in Christ Jesus" (Philippians 4:6–7). When we pray, God will give us His peace, and that peace will help us in the time of waiting. There's a worldly peace and a godly peace. Worldly peace never really satisfies and is based on favorable circumstances. Godly peace is lasting and remains despite the circumstances you're facing. It's a sincere reliance and trust in God that He will work everything out in His timing, especially the circumstances outside your control (Romans 8:28). Jesus didn't receive His desired answer to His prayer, but He trusted His life to God to do His will. God is likely to answer your prayer in one of three ways: yes, no, and not yet. Sometimes He has something better in store for you than what you're asking for, but requires you to wait. You may not receive the desired outcome to your prayer, but God always hears you, "Then you will call on me and come and pray to me, and I will listen to you" (Jeremiah 29:12). When you give Him your anxiety, He gives you His peace. In turn, His peace will guard your heart and mind from the concern and grief of the situation you're in. Always know that He understands and knows exactly what you're going through and where you are in life.

"For I know the plans I have for you," declares the Lord, "plans to prosper you and not to harm you, plans to give you hope and a future." (Jeremiah 29:11)

A Father's Love

Neither death nor life, neither angels nor demons, neither the present nor the future, nor any powers, neither height nor depth, nor anything else in all creation, will be able to separate us from the love of God that is in Christ Jesus our Lord. (Romans 8:38–39)

You are God's precious child. You were uniquely created by Him. There is no one like you in the world, truly one of a kind, made for a purpose, not simply to just exist, "For we are God's handiwork, created in Christ Jesus to do good works, which God prepared in advance for us to do" (Ephesians 2:10). That purpose is revealed when we draw near to God and enter into a relationship with Him. The more you know God, the more you will know yourself, and who God truly made you to be. He will reveal to you the reason you were created. Since God created you, wouldn't He know what is best for you, even though you may think or feel otherwise? Human understanding and knowledge are limited. Human feelings are fickle and unstable no matter how strong you think they are. God sees the bigger picture, even when we can't make sense of it all. His greatest desire, apart from wanting you to spend eternity with Him, is for you to fulfill your God-given purpose. There are so many different teachings and agendas in this world that will keep you from your ultimate purpose. You can still accomplish things separate from God—many people do—but are their full potential being reached? Many lack, even after they've accomplished their worldly goals and dreams. God has an amazing plan for you and He simply wants the best for you, "What no eye has seen, what no ear has heard, and what no human mind has conceived—the things God has prepared for those who love him" (1 Corinthians 2:9).

God's love is evident throughout scripture. I could reference many biblical texts, but I'd like to focus on two stories. The first story is of a woman Jesus healed from a long-term sickness.

"A large crowd followed and pressed around him. And a woman was there who had been subject to bleeding for twelve years. She had suffered a great deal under the care of many doctors and had spent all she had, yet instead of getting better she grew worse. When she heard about Jesus, she came up behind him in the crowd and touched his cloak, because she thought, 'If I just touch his clothes, I will be healed.' Immediately her bleeding stopped and she felt in her body that she was freed from her suffering. At once Jesus realized that power had gone out from him. He turned around in the crowd and asked, 'Who touched my clothes?' 'You see the people crowding against you,' his disciples answered, 'and yet you can ask, Who touched me?'

But Jesus kept looking around to see who had done it. Then the woman, knowing what had happened to her, came and fell at His feet and, trembling with fear, told him the whole truth. He said to her, 'Daughter, your faith has healed you. Go in peace and be freed from your suffering'" (Mark 5:24–34).

This woman was an outcast, deemed unclean by society because of her debilitating illness. According to her culture, she was an untouchable because of her constant bleeding. She had spent all she had on trying to cure her illness and was most likely homeless because no one, not even her own family, would accept her for what she had become. She suffered greatly, not just from the physical pain but the emotional pain of being unloved, having not heard any words of endearment toward her for the past twelve years. She was most likely to have been taunted and teased. But Jesus did not tell her to go away; He saw her great physical and emotional need. As He acknowledges her, He calls her "daughter." This is the only scripturally recorded term of endearment uttered by Jesus, and it was said to someone the world had despised and rejected. This would have been the first time she would have heard an endearing term directed at her in twelve years. Not only did Jesus heal her physical pain, but He also healed her emotional pain. By calling her daughter, He removed any self-doubt and instilled a sense of dignity and value that even if no one else in the world saw her as precious, He did. The world may judge you, look down on you, reject you, and close friends and family may have mistreated you, but your heavenly father sees you, knows you, and loves you immensely. Nothing and no one can stop His love for you.

The second story is the well-known parable of the Prodigal Son, also known as the Lost Son.

"There was a man who had two sons. The younger one said to his father, 'Father, give me my share of the estate.' So he divided his property between them. Not long after that, the younger son got together all he had, set off for a distant country and there squandered his wealth in wild living. After he had spent everything, there was a severe famine in that whole country, and he began to be in need. So he went and hired himself out to a citizen of that country, who sent him to his fields to feed pigs. He longed to fill his stomach with the pods that the pigs were eating, but no one gave him anything. When he came to his senses, he said, 'How many of my father's hired servants have food to spare, and here I am starving to death! I will set out and go back to my father and say to him: Father, I have sinned against heaven and against you. I am no longer worthy to be called your son; make me like one of your hired servants.' So he got up and went to his father. But while he was still a long way off, his father saw him and was filled with compassion for

him; he ran to his son, threw his arms around him and kissed him. The son said to him, 'Father, I have sinned against heaven and against you. I am no longer worthy to be called your son.' But the father said to his servants, 'Quick! Bring the best robe and put it on him. Put a ring on his finger and sandals on his feet. Bring the fattened calf and kill it. Let's have a feast and celebrate. For this son of mine was dead and is alive again; he was lost and is found.' So they began to celebrate" (Luke 15:11–24).

The son demands his inherence. This was an insult to the father and was culturally unacceptable. It's like saying to the father, "I wish you were dead." Surprisingly, the father granted his request when he had every right to kick him out of his home and punish him. The rebellious son goes off and squanders his newfound wealth in wild living and loses everything he inherited. He comes to his senses and, filled with remorse, heads back home to his father to beg to be accepted as a slave. The father looks out on the horizon and sees his son, and although the story doesn't say it, I wouldn't be surprised if he looked for his son every day. Recognizing his figure and saunter, the father, filled with compassion, ran to him, hugged, and kissed him. He ran to the son that rejected him. In that culture, men didn't run; it was seen as undignified. But this father didn't care; his son was lost and is now found. In effect, he was saying, "It doesn't matter what you've done, I love you more." The son admits his sin against his father. Apart from his confession, the father sees his repentance by his act of humility, returning to the father, seeking his care and love. The father does something even more amazing. He asks his servants to bring the best robe and put it on him, to put a ring on his finger and sandals on his feet. You see, the best robe would have been the father's own robe, thus wrapping the son in the father's love and restoring his identity. The ring would have been a signet ring with the family seal, meaning he represented the family once again and had equal authority in the family business. The sandals differentiated someone as a slave or a child; household slaves typically didn't wear sandals. The father, by his actions, is reinstating his son as an heir. He then asked for the fatted calf that was being prepared for a momentous occasion to be used for his son's return. He saw it as his son coming back to life from the dead, and there was a great feast and celebration.

In that time, when a son shamed and rebelled against their father's authority, a cultural ceremony was conducted by the family, involving the community. This would mean the child was forever banished from that family and community. That's probably why the father ran to the son, to get to him first before anyone else could. He quickly asked for the robe, ring, and sandals to be brought to them so the community could see and understand that the father accepted his son back. The feast wasn't just a celebration of the son's return but a further show of acceptance to the community that this child of his who rejected him was now received back as child and heir.

An amazing act of mercy, love, and forgiveness by the father. He didn't lecture the child or bring him down in any way. He accepted his child back with open arms despite the disrespect he showed to him. If we're honest, we've all been the prodigal at some point. We may not have gone as far as the son did in this story, but there were times we rebelled against God in our own way.

This isn't just a nice story about a father and his wayward child. When Jesus told this parable, He spoke about God, the Father. You see, the father in this story is God, and the prodigal child is you; it's me; it's every man, woman, and child. No matter how far you've strayed from God, you can always return to Him. He's there, waiting for you to return, but you've got to take the first step and turn your heart toward Him, and the moment you do that, He comes running to you.

Here's a story that contrasts the sincere love of God as a father:

> You have a child. When she reaches the age of comprehension, you explain to her, "I will set many rules for you to follow. Every single one must be obeyed. I expect you to excel in your education

and receive nothing less than an A on every exam. Do not ever embarrass me or shame my name. I want you to gain a profession in the upper echelons of society—a lawyer, a doctor, or a politician. On my deathbed, I will review your life. If you follow my requests to the letter, I will accept you as my child."

What type of parent would treat their child this way? Many words come to mind, but manipulative and unloving would be a start. A loving parent would not treat their child this way. It's certainly not how God treats us. His love for us is not based on our performance. He loves us simply because He is our father, and we are His children. It doesn't matter what you have done; you are and always will be God's child. In the story of the Prodigal Son, I think it's quite significant that the father would run to the son and not the other way around. It's the only imagery written in the Bible of our heavenly father running, and he's not running to a perfect, sinless child; rather, he is running to a rebellious child, someone you wouldn't think deserves the father's love or attention. But God, our Father, doesn't see the sins and mistakes; He sees His precious child. The son thinks he will return as a slave because of the error of his ways, but the father is saying, "No, you are my dear child, an heir to all my glory." This is the unfathomable, unconditional love of our heavenly father.

See what great love the Father has lavished on us, that we should be called children of God! And that is what we are! (1 John 3:1)

God's Sacrifice

This is love: not that we loved God, but that he loved us and sent his Son as an atoning sacrifice for our sins. (1 John 4:10)

Jesus was sent to Earth for a specific purpose. He still had a choice, to accept that purpose or to walk away from it. The Devil tried to stop Jesus from fulfilling His purpose. He tempted Jesus (Matthew 4:1–11). A sinless sacrifice was required. If Jesus gave in to any of these temptations, He would have been unable to fulfil His purpose. But Jesus resisted the Devil's schemes.

Jesus had the option of an easy road. He could have lived a pain-free life, void of hardship, torture, and unimaginable heartbreak. I can't imagine what it would be like to bear the sin of all humanity. Jesus could have walked away from being mocked and humiliated, and instead live a life of prosperity and kingship on Earth as offered by the Devil. However, Jesus chose the difficult way. Why? I would be hard-pressed to find anyone who would want to purposely take the difficult road full of hardship and suffering. Jesus chose the difficult way because, firstly, He had a close relationship with God, the Father. Jesus knew what God wanted Him to do and He wanted to do the Father's will. It was difficult for Him, He asked the

Father to take away the suffering (Luke 22:42), yet Jesus trusted the Father to fulfill the ultimate plan in His life. Secondly, Jesus chose the difficult way because He loves us deeply. He couldn't bear to spend life, both now and in eternity, without us. He was thinking of you, me, and everyone else while on the cross.

God showed the ultimate expression of love, for it was while we were still sinners that Jesus died for us (Romans 5:8). God is the ultimate pursuer. There are many in the world today that don't know God, or have turned their back on God. Yet He hasn't turned away from them. He gently pursues until their last breath. On the cross, Jesus showed incredible love and mercy for the very people that crucified Him, He prayed: "Father, forgive them, for they do not know what they are doing" (Luke 23:34). It's amazing what God did for us. Here's a story to put it into perspective:

> Imagine you have a son that you absolutely cherish and adore, with a love you cannot put into words. He's obedient, loving, kind, and caring. He has such a beautiful heart and soul. You find out that your son is being bullied. This bully doesn't like your son and makes life difficult for him; in fact, he makes attempts to harm your son. It greatly distresses him and in turn evokes all sorts of emotions in you.

> After some time of this bully making your son live through daily physical and emotional torment, the bully is in an accident and loses a considerable amount of blood. Without a blood transfusion, he won't pull through. The bully has a rare blood type not readily available. You realize that your son has the same rare blood type. The only way for that bully to live is if you allow your son's life to be sacrificed so that your son's blood can be given to this bully to live.

I won't bother asking what you would do. I'm sure it would be the same thing I would do, and that would be nothing. There is absolutely no way I would sacrifice my child, who I cherish and love dearly, to keep that bully alive. I wouldn't even entertain that thought for a second. Yet, that is what God, our father, did for us. Even though we've done wrong, even though we rebelled against Him in different ways, He still sent His son Jesus for us so we can have a relationship with Him.

You might say, "No decent, loving, and caring parent would sacrifice their child, so what does this say about God?" Remember, Jesus is God in human form. In effect, God came down to Earth himself in the form of Jesus, so it's like God sacrificed himself for us. Also, God wouldn't have let His son be tortured and crucified without redemption. God's plan, after the fulfillment of Jesus' purpose on Earth, was to always resurrect Jesus and bring Him back home to be with Him.

Greater love has no one than this: to lay down one's life for one's friends. (John 15:13)

Why did God come down to Earth? Because only He could do what was required to save us. He stepped down from a perfect paradise and got His hands dirty so that we could spend eternity with Him.

God came from a place of perfection, peace, and joy. A place free of trouble, pain, and suffering. When God came down to Earth, He stepped into our vulnerability and fragility. He didn't take the form of a kingly ruler, a military leader, or a persuasive and powerful politician. He came down to Earth the same way as everyone else: as a baby. He wasn't born into influence or affluence; He was born into poverty. He wasn't born in a royal palace but in a stable. The way God came down to Earth makes a huge declaration. He had every right to be surrounded by privilege and power, having come from a place of perfection and abundance. Yet God self-sacrificed like no one ever has. He gave up everything to identify with you and to show you how much He loves you and wants to have a relationship with you.

He's not some distant deity that's apathetic; He is relational and desires our love. Here's a story that may better explain what God did for us:

> Imagine you are the wealthiest person in the world. You have a plethora of servants at your beck and call. You're known to uphold the highest form of dignified living and considered by many to be in a higher class of humanity due to your prestige and affluence. While working from home one day, you keep an eye on your children playing in the garden. You're intensely focused on your work when you suddenly hear one of your children scream in terror. You quickly look out the window. Your son lies motionless on the ground in the mud. It seems he climbed the oak tree and has fallen. You've warned them often not to climb the trees or play near the muddy patch.

What would you do in that instant? Would you say to yourself, "Well, I told them not to climb the tree," and leave your son lying there unconscious? Would you call one of your servants to check on your son to ensure he is well? Or would you run to your son as fast as possible, get on your knees in the mud, and take him in your arms and help him in every way possible? Any loving parent would react in the third instance, and God is no different. He came down to us to heal us and save us. He stepped out of the perfection of Heaven and got dirty with worldly pain, weakness, and suffering of the human condition for our sake. God's love is different from the love we give. Think of the deepest ocean trench, which is but a shallow pond to God. Think of the length of the deepest cave to the top of the world, which is but an inch to God—or how about as far as the east is from the west, which goes on and on.

It's an amazing truth that the Creator of the universe, God Almighty, calls you His child and wants you to call Him father. God, the Father, sent His beloved son for you so that He might gain your love and that you might call Him father. Jesus said that God loves you as much as He loves Him (John 17:23). His love is everlasting, and nothing will ever separate you from the love of God. "He who did not spare His own Son, but gave Him up for us all—how will He not also, along with Him, graciously give us all things?" (Romans 8:32). God, the Father, is there for you every moment of your life. He knows the world can be challenging. He experienced worldly suffering—He knows, empathizes, and cares.

There's a story that sums up God's love for each of us. It's not in scripture, but it has a ring of truth about it:

You and Jesus are alone. You soon realize that you are the only two people in the world. You take this opportunity to ask Jesus a question, "Jesus, besides yourself, I seem to be the only other person in the world. How much do you love me?" Jesus looks at you with compassion and replies, "This much." Then He stretches out His arms and gives His life.

If you were the only person in the world, God still would have sent His only son Jesus to give His life just for you! That's how much God loves you; you are His precious child, and don't ever forget it!

www.ingramcontent.com/pod-product-compliance
Lightning Source LLC
Chambersburg PA
CBHW022020290426
44109CB00015B/1244